COUNTRY

Formal Name: Republic of Kenya.

Short Form: Kenya.

Term for Citizen(s): Kenyan(s).

Capital: Nairobi.

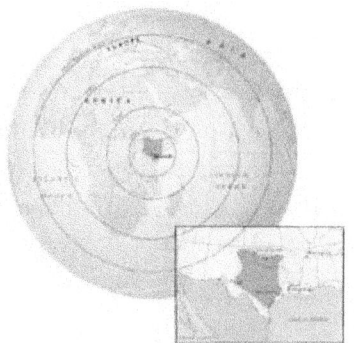

Click to Enlarge Image

Major Cities: The country's largest cites are Nairobi, the capital and chief manufacturing center; Mombasa, the principal seaport; and Kisumu, the chief port on Lake Victoria. Smaller cities include Nakuru, a commercial and manufacturing center in the Eastern Rift Valley; and Eldoret, an industrial center in western Kenya. The population of cities, according to the 1999 census, was Nairobi, 1,346,000; Mombasa, 465,000; Kisumu, 185,000; Nakuru, 163,000; and Eldoret, 105,000.

Independence: December 12, 1963, from the United Kingdom.

Public Holidays: New Year's Day (January 1); Good Friday (movable date in March or April); Easter Monday (movable date in March or April); Labor Day (May 1); Madaraka Day, which celebrates self-government (June 1); Moi Day (October 10); Kenyatta Forces Day (October 20); Eid al Fitr (movable date according to the Islamic calendar); Jamhuri/Independence Day (December 12); Christmas Day (December 25); and Boxing Day (December 26).

Flag: Kenya's flag features three equal horizontal bands of black (top), red, and green; the red band is edged in white. Centered on the flag is a large warrior's shield covering crossed spears.

Click to Enlarge Image

HISTORICAL BACKGROUND

Prehistory and Early History: Eastern Africa may have provided the setting for the earliest development of the human species. Archaeologists working in the Rift Valley region, beginning with Mary and Louis Leakey in the 1930s, have unearthed fossils of several species of protohumans dating to as much as 20 million years ago. Recent finds near Kenya's Lake Turkana indicate that hominids lived in the area 2.6 million years ago. Ancestors of modern Kenya's population began arriving in the region around 2000 B.C., when Cushitic-speaking pastoralists migrated south from the Ethiopia highlands. Between 500 B.C. and A.D. 500, Nilotic speakers arrived, along with Bantu-speaking peoples, who now make up three-quarters of Kenya's population.

On Kenya's coast, trade with the nearby Arabian Peninsula was well-established by A.D. 100. In the medieval period, Arabs settled on the coast, establishing several autonomous city-states (including Mombasa, Malindi, and Pate) ruled by sultans. As Arabs and the local Bantu-speaking tribes intermarried, a distinct civilization and a new language emerged, a mixture of Arabic and Bantu, called Swahili. Swahili became the lingua franca of the coastal trade that exchanged trade goods from Kenya's interior—animal skins, ivory and horn, agricultural produce, and slaves—for goods from the Middle East and even the Far East. Arab dominance on the coast was eclipsed by the arrival in 1498 of the Portuguese, whose control gave way in turn to renewed Arab control under the Imam of Oman in the 1600s. In the mid-nineteenth century, British influence superseded that of the Arabs. Unlike their Arab predecessors, the British showed interest in controlling land beyond the coastal region and encouraged European explorers to map the interior.

Colonial Era: British colonial control of Kenya dates from the Berlin Conference of 1885, when the European powers partitioned East Africa into spheres of influence, with present-day Kenya passing to the British. Beginning in 1895, a railroad was built from Mombasa to Kisumu on Lake Victoria in order to facilitate trade with the interior and with Uganda. The British government established the East African Protectorate and in 1920 made Kenya a British crown colony. The British opened the fertile highlands to white settlers, who established themselves as large-scale farmers. Extensive tracts of the best land were taken from Africans and reserved for white settlers, who eventually gained control of the colonial government. The white settler-dominated government denied the dispossessed Africans political participation, restricted their cultivation of cash crops such as coffee, permitted forced labor, and maintained a "white highlands" policy that restricted the Kikuyu, one of the largest tribes, to overcrowded reserves. Other tribes and non-whites such as East Indians also faced restrictions.

Protest by Africans, which began in the 1920s, peaked between 1952 and 1956 with the so-called "Mau-Mau" Emergency, an armed Kikuyu-led insurrection directed against white settler domination and British colonial rule. The British put Kenya under a state of emergency until 1959 and imprisoned many of the colony's nationalist leaders, including Jomo Kenyatta, a British-educated Kikuyu and an activist since the 1920s. After the Mau-Mau revolt abated, Britain increased African representation in the colony's legislative council until, in 1961, there was an African majority. Kenya became independent on December 12, 1963, and the next year became a republic and joined the Commonwealth. Kenyatta, head of the Kenya African National Union (KANU), became Kenya's first president.

Independence under Kenyatta: Kenyatta engineered successive measures that increased the powers vested in the presidency, giving the executive, for example, the power to detain political opponents without trial if they posed a threat to public order. By 1969, KANU was the sole political party in a de facto one-party state. To forestall opposition and tribal conflict, Kenyatta relied on largesse, dispensing offices—with all the wealth such patronage entailed—across ethnic groups. In the economy, he pursued pro-Western, essentially free-market capitalist policies. Seeking to stem the outflow of capital underway since 1961, he backed policies favorable to foreign investors and conciliated white settlers (55,000 in 1962). Foreign investors were free to remit profits and to own property, albeit sometimes on condition of some government co-ownership. Whites were guaranteed ownership rights to land and to compensation if they chose to leave. Kenyatta supported the distribution of white settler land to Africans through land purchase and struck a deal with Britain to help finance a massive land purchase. This "Africanization" of land included the transfer of more than 6,070 square kilometers of land to a group of well-connected Kenyans, mainly Kikuyu, and fostered the emergence of a new privileged class of African plantation owners. To counter criticism for catering to the privileged, Kenyatta also backed the distribution to Africans of hundreds of thousands of smallholdings and spent a third of the national budget on education. These policies brought sufficiently widespread improvement in living standards to ensure continuing support for the government.

Under Kenyatta's presidency, Kenya's economic performance was better than most in Africa. The rate of economic growth was among the highest on the continent. Despite severe drought, two oil shocks, ethnic conflicts, and border skirmishes, Kenya's gross national product grew on average at more than 6 percent a year, almost fivefold from 1971 to 1981. At the same time, the economy remained heavily dependent on a limited range of primary commodity exports and highly vulnerable to fluctuations in world commodity prices. Growth also generated tremendous disparities of wealth, much of which was in the hands of Kenyatta's family and close associates. This concentration of wealth, along with an extremely high rate of population growth, meant that most Kenyans did not realize a correspondingly large increase in per capita well-being under Kenyatta's leadership.

The Moi Presidency and the Kibaki Government: At Kenyatta's death at age 86 in August 1978, Vice President Daniel arap Moi succeeded him as president. Popular at first, Moi promised to tackle corruption, limit foreign ownership of industry, review his predecessor's land allocation policies and the self-enrichment of the ruling group, and abolish primary school fees. As a deteriorating economy necessitated austerity measures and aroused opposition, however, Moi began to follow in Kenyatta's autocratic footsteps. In June 1982, the ruling party, KANU, had the National Assembly amend the constitution to make Kenya officially a one-party state and KANU the sole legal party. The same year, Moi weathered a coup attempt by junior ranks of the air force, 1,000 of whom he court-martialed. To discourage opposition, he dismantled the air force and closed the universities for a time. Throughout the 1980s, he further tightened political control even as corruption spread among his cohorts. Eventually, Western powers and international financial donor agencies balked at continuing to provide Kenya with vital financial aid. By the 1990s, they intermittently suspended grants and loans, pending political and economic reforms and improvement in the records on human rights and corruption. In 1991 Moi finally bowed to pressure from donors and opposition groups and agreed to an amendment reinstating multiparty elections. In 1992, in the first multiparty elections in 26 years, the ethnically fractured opposition failed to dislodge Moi and KANU from power. Moi also held onto power in the 1997 elections, amid charges of electoral fraud, rampant corruption, and lack of public safety, and despite ongoing deterioration in many economic indicators. Moi's fifth and final term was marked by continuing suspensions of donor aid and the first proof of Kenya's vulnerability to international terrorism, the August 1998 bombing of the U.S. Embassy in Nairobi.

Forced under the constitution to retire in December 2002, Moi engineered the nomination of Uhuru Kenyatta, son of Kenya's first leader, as KANU's candidate for president. Mwai Kibaki, who ran against Moi in 1992 and 1997 and once was his vice president, was the candidate of the multiethnic, united opposition group, the National Rainbow Coalition (NARC). Kibaki won decisively, and NARC achieved a solid parliamentary majority on an anticorruption platform. The election, although not free of vote-rigging, was the most credible since independence.

Kibaki immediately faced major challenges in holding the ruling NARC together. The constituent parties of NARC were divided over drafts for a new constitution, which contained various controversial proposals, including, for example, a new office of prime minister, an upper chamber of parliament, devolution of powers to district level, and constitutional recognition of Islamic courts. In 2005 the NARC coalition splintered over the constitutional review process, with defectors joining with KANU to form a new opposition coalition, the Orange Democratic Movement. The opposition defeated the government's final draft constitution in a popular referendum in November 2005. Discussions about a new constitution are continuing in the run-up to the 2007 elections, in which Kibaki is expected to run for a second term as the candidate of the new NARC–Kenya party.

Apart from the challenge of achieving cross-party consensus on a new constitution, the Kibaki administration has faced long-standing problems inherited from Kibaki's predecessor—a sluggish agriculture-based economy, rundown infrastructure, poverty rates exceeding 50 percent, endemic corruption, spiraling crime, and a heavy burden of disease, including human immunodeficiency virus/acquired immune deficiency syndrome (HIV/AIDS). In addition, Kenya has seen growing ethnic tensions between coastal Muslims and other Kenyans about the former's perceived exclusion from power. Also, new acts of terrorism in Mombasa alarmed authorities in November 2003, prompting travel advisories by Western governments.

The early months of the Kibaki administration witnessed much progress, with the introduction of universal free primary education, the adoption of anticorruption measures, and a cleanup of the judiciary, as well as a resumption of robust economic growth after a long period of stagnation. International financial institutions, which had suspended development assistance in previous years, gave the new administration an early vote of confidence by resuming aid. Already by 2004, however, disenchantment with the Kibaki administration had set in when progress against corruption stalled and no legal action against Moi and his cronies was undertaken. Kenya's competent and honest anticorruption tsar, John Githongo, resigned in February 2005 and fled to the United Kingdom (UK), citing threats. He also complained of interference with investigations of high-level graft by government ministers and other scandals. Western goodwill toward Kenya dissipated, prompting the United States, Germany, and the Netherlands to cut back on aid and the UK, Kenya's largest foreign investor, to slow investment. Donor country and investor wariness added to other woes, including a drought—the worst since 1971—that by January 2006 had put 2.5 million Kenyans at risk of starvation. Since 2006, because of conflict in neighboring Somalia, Kenya has also faced increasing pressure from refugees.

GEOGRAPHY

Location: Kenya lies astride the equator in Eastern Africa between Somalia and Tanzania and bordering the Indian Ocean.

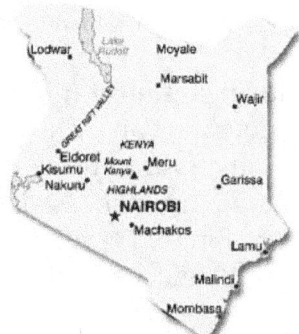

Size: The total area of 582,650 square kilometers (somewhat larger than France) includes 13,400 square kilometers of water, mainly in Lake Turkana (also known as Lake Rudolf) and Kenya's portion of Lake Victoria.

Click to Enlarge Image

Land Boundaries: Kenya's land boundaries total 3,477 kilometers. The country is bounded by Ethiopia (861 kilometers), Somalia (682 kilometers), Sudan (232 kilometers), Tanzania (769 kilometers), and Uganda (933 kilometers).

Length of Coastline: Kenya has 536 kilometers of coastline on the Indian Ocean.

Maritime Claims: Kenya's territorial sea extends 12 nautical miles. The exclusive economic (fishing) zone is 200 nautical miles, and the continental shelf extends to a 200-meter depth or to the depth of exploitation.

Topography: Kenya rises from a low coastal plain on the Indian Ocean in a series of plateaus to more than 3,000 meters in the center of the country. An inland region of semi-arid, bush-covered plains constitutes most of the country's land area. In the northwest, high-lying scrublands straddle Lake Turkana (Lake Rudolf) and the Kulal Mountains. In the southwest lie the fertile grasslands and forests of the Kenya Highlands, one of the most successful agricultural production regions in Africa. North of Nairobi, the Kenya Highlands is bisected by the Great Rift Valley, an irregular depression that cuts through western Kenya from north to south in two branches. The Rift Valley is the location of the country's highest mountains, including, in the eastern section, the snow-capped Mt. Kenya (5,199 meters), the country's highest point and Africa's second highest. In the south, mountain plains descend westward to the shores of Lake Victoria.

Principal Rivers: Kenya's principal rivers are the 710-kilometer-long Tana, and the Athi, both flowing southeast to the Indian Ocean. Other rivers include the Ewaso Ngiro, flowing northeast to the swamps of the Lorian Plain, and the Nzoia, Yala, and Gori, which drain into Lake Victoria.

Climate: Kenya's climate varies from tropical along the coast to arid in the interior, especially in the north and northeast. Intermittent droughts affect most of the country. Less than 15 percent of the country receives somewhat reliable rainfall of 760 millimeters or more per year, mainly the southwestern highlands near Lake Victoria and the coastal area, which is tempered by monsoon winds. Most of the country experiences two wet and two dry seasons. The driest month is August, with 24 millimeters average rainfall, and the wettest is April, the period of "long rains," with 266 millimeters. The hottest month is February, with temperatures of 13°C to 28°C, and the coolest is July, with temperatures of 11°C to 23°C. The highlands feature a bracing temperate climate. Nairobi, at an elevation of 1,820 meters, has a very pleasant climate throughout the year.

Natural Resources: Kenya's most valuable natural assets are rich agricultural land and a unique physiography and wildlife. The highly diverse wildlife is a key draw for the tourism industry. The country is not well endowed with mineral resources. Mineral resources currently exploited are gold, limestone, soda ash, salt, rubies, fluorspar, and garnets. At present, only 3 percent of the land is forested, a reduction by half over the past three decades. Kenya's water resources are similarly under pressure. Kenya relies to a significant extent on hydropower.

Land Use: Of Kenya's land surface, between 7 and 8 percent is arable, while slightly less than 1 percent is in permanent crops. According to a 1998 estimate, irrigated land totaled about 670 square kilometers.

Environmental Factors: Kenya faces serious interrelated environmental problems, including deforestation, soil erosion, desertification, water shortage and degraded water quality, poaching, and domestic and industrial pollution. Water resources are under pressure from agricultural chemicals and urban and industrial wastes, as well as from use for hydroelectric power. A shortage of water is expected to pose a problem in the coming years. Water-quality problems in lakes, including water hyacinth infestation in Lake Victoria, have contributed to a substantial decline in fishing output and endangered fish species. Output from forestry also has declined because of resource degradation. Overexploitation over the past three decades has reduced the country's timber resources by one-half. At present only 3 percent of the land remains forested, and an estimated 5,000 hectares of forest are lost each year. This loss of forest aggravates erosion, the silting of dams and flooding, and the loss of biodiversity. In response to ecological disruption, activists have pressed with some success for policies that encourage sustainable resource use. The 2004 Nobel Peace Prize went to the Kenyan environmentalist, Wangari Maathai, best known for organizing a grassroots movement in which thousands of people were mobilized over the years to plant 30 million trees in Kenya and elsewhere and to protest forest clearance for luxury development. Imprisoned as an opponent of President Moi, Maathai linked deforestation with the plight of rural women, who are forced to spend untold hours in search of scarce firewood and water.

Time Zone: Kenya lies in one time zone, which is three hours ahead of Greenwich Mean Time Standard Time (GMT + 3). Kenya does not operate daylight saving time.

SOCIETY

Population: In 2007 Kenya's population was estimated at 36,913,721, up from 28.7 million reported in the 1999 national census and from 15.3 million in the 1979 census. In 2006 the annual population growth rate was about 2.8 percent, a rate substantially below that of the early 1980s, when Kenya's growth reached 4 percent, the highest rate in the world. As of the end of 2006, Kenya was host to some 220,000 refugees from neighboring countries, including 162,000 from Somalia and most of the remainder from Sudan. Somewhat more than one-third of Kenya's population lives in urban areas, with the greatest concentration in Nairobi. The non-city-dwelling population is also heavily concentrated in areas of fertile land in the center and west of the country. The country's population density is about 59 people per square kilometer, with extremely uneven distribution.

Demography: Kenya was the first sub-Saharan African country to adopt a national family planning program and one of a small handful to undergo a demographic transition to much lower fertility. Since the late 1970s, contraceptive prevalence has doubled, and the total fertility rate in Kenya has fallen from 8.0 children per woman to about half that number. Current estimates on fertility range from 3.1 to 5 births per woman. Kenya now has a birthrate that is among the lowest in sub-Saharan Africa, at between 28 and 39 per 1,000 population (2007 estimate). At the same time, according to various 2005 to 2007 estimates, life expectancy at birth has fallen to between 47 and 55 years. Current estimates place the death rate at between 11 and 16 deaths per 1,000 population and infant mortality rate at 57 to 74 per 1,000 live births. The mortality rate among children under five was 120 per 1,000 births in 2004, up from 96 per 1,000 in 1970. The age structure of the population is very young, with 42 percent of the population under age 15 and only 2.6 percent 65 or older. The median age is 18.6 years.

Ethnic Groups and Languages: People of African descent make up about 97 percent of the population; they are divided into about 40 ethnic groups belonging to three linguistic families: Bantu, Cushitic, and Nilotic. Bantu-speaking Kenyans comprise three groups: western (Luhya), highlands (including the Kikuyu and the Kamba), and coastal (Mijikenda) Bantu. The major groups of Nilotic speakers are the river–lake (Luo), highlands (Kalenjin), and plains or eastern (Masai). The Cushitic-speaking groups include the Oromo and Somali. The Kikuyu, who make up 22 percent of the population, constitute Kenya's largest ethnic group. The next largest groups are the Luhya (14 percent), Luo (13 percent), Kalenjin (12 percent), and Kamba (11 percent). Additional groups include the Kisii (6 percent), Meru (6 percent), and other African (15 percent). Small numbers of people of Indian, Pakistani, and European descent live in the interior, and there are some Arabs along the coast. The official languages of Kenya are Swahili and English; many indigenous languages from the three language families also are spoken.

Religion: About three-quarters of Kenyans profess some form of Christianity, although fewer are affiliated with a church. About 40 to 45 percent of Kenyans are Protestant, while 30 percent are Roman Catholic. Estimates for the percentage of the population that adheres to indigenous beliefs and to Islam vary widely, ranging from 10 to 25 percent for the former and 7 to 20 percent for Muslims. One percent are Hindus and Sikhs. The population includes very few professed atheists.

Education and Literacy: Estimates of the Kenyan literacy rate range between 75 and 85 percent, with the female rate about 10 points lower than the male. The education system, beset by non-enrollment and low completion rates, offers eight years of compulsory primary education, beginning at age six, four years of secondary school, and four years of university education. The language of instruction from the secondary stage onward is English. Primary enrollment since 2002 has included about 75 percent of children. This enrollment rate remains below the nearly 100 percent rate in the 1980s prior to the introduction, under donor pressure, of user fees. The primary school completion rate in 2002 was less than one-half. Primary school enrollment has increased under the Kibaki government, which immediately fulfilled its campaign pledge to abolish user charges and special fees. The government now offers universal free primary education, a change from earlier cost-sharing arrangements between the government and parents. Secondary school enrollment in 2002 included only about 23 percent of the relevant age-group and remains low. Greater government expenditure on education—more than 8 percent of gross domestic product and 30 percent of current government spending in 2004—promises to reverse the declining trend in educational standards, as well as to increase the fiscal deficit.

Kenya has five public universities and about twice that many private institutions of higher education. Since the 1980s, there has been a tremendous expansion in universities in response to high demand. The public universities are the University of Nairobi (founded in 1956); Kenyatta University (1972), in Nairobi; the Jomo Kenyatta University of Agriculture and Technology (1981), near Nairobi; Egerton University (1939), near Nakuru; and Moi University (1984), outside Eldoret. The government also provides opportunities for higher education through several polytechnic institutes and several dozen teacher-training colleges.

Health: Tropical diseases, especially malaria, and tuberculosis have long been a public health problem in Kenya. In recent years, infection with the human immunodeficiency virus (HIV), which causes acquired immune deficiency syndrome (AIDS), also has become a severe problem. Estimates of the incidence of infection differ widely. The United Nations Development Programme (UNDP) claimed in 2006 that more than 16 percent of adults in Kenya are HIV-infected, whereas the Joint United Nations Programme on HIV/AIDS (UNAIDS) cites the much lower figure of 6.7 percent. Despite politically charged disputes over the numbers, however, the Kenyan government recently declared HIV/AIDS a national disaster. In 2004 the Kenyan Ministry of Health announced that HIV/AIDS had surpassed malaria and tuberculosis as the leading disease killer in the country. Thanks largely to AIDS, life expectancy in Kenya has dropped by about a decade. Since 1984 more than 1.5 million Kenyans have died because of HIV/AIDS. More than 3 million Kenyans are HIV positive. More than 70 people a day die of HIV-related illnesses. The prevalence rate for women is nearly twice that for men. The rate of orphanhood stands at about 11 percent. AIDS has contributed significantly to Kenya's dismal ranking in the latest UNDP *Human Development Report*, whose Human Development Index (HDI) score is an amalgam of gross domestic product per head, figures for life expectancy, adult literacy, and school enrollment. The 2006 report ranked Kenya 152nd out of 177 countries on the HDI and pointed out that Kenya is one of the world's worst performers in infant mortality. Estimates of the infant mortality rate range from 57 to 74 deaths/1,000 live births. The maternal mortality ratio is also among the highest in the world, thanks in part to female genital cutting, illegal since 2001 for girls under 16.

Apart from major disease killers, Kenya has a serious problem with accidental death, specifically by motor vehicles. Kenya has the highest rate of road accidents in the world, with 510 fatal accidents per 100,000 vehicles (2004 estimate), as compared to second-ranked South Africa, with 260 fatalities, and the United Kingdom, with 20. In February 2004, in an attempt to improve Kenya's appalling record, the government obliged the owners of the country's 25,000 *matutas* (minibuses), the backbone of public transportation, to install new safety equipment on their vehicles. Investment in road projects also is planned.

Kenya's health infrastructure suffers from urban-rural and regional imbalances, lack of investment, and a personnel shortage, with, for example, one doctor for 10,150 people (as of 2000).

Welfare: Over the past several decades, Kenya has seen declining income per head and growing disparities of income and wealth. Various estimates between 2000 and 2006 stated that the top decile of the population enjoyed 37 to 42 percent of income, while the lowest decile had only 1 to 2 percent. The number of people living below the poverty line (as defined in Kenya) is estimated to have increased from 11.3 million (48.4 percent of the population) in 1990 to 17.1 million (55.4 percent of the population) in 2001. Despite high and growing levels of poverty, social protection is only now becoming a priority in Kenya. Hitherto, the country has not had social welfare or protection provisions that reach workers in both the formal and informal sectors. Plans are now underway to extend basic income replacement support measures and other protections to more workers. The Kenyan government is converting its existing 2.9 million-member National Social Security Fund (NSSF), a provident fund for private-sector workers, into a more comprehensive national social insurance pension plan. Under a draft NSSF Act Amendment Bill, eligibility will extend to any person with a monthly or seasonal income. The new benefits will include lifetime old-age, invalid, and survivors' pensions, a maternity grant, and a funeral grant.

In addition, the National Health Insurance Fund (NHIF) is slated to be restructured to provide universal compulsory social health insurance coverage for every citizen. Legislation for a new system, the National Social Health Insurance Scheme, was passed in 2005 but was held up by President Kibaki, citing financial issues. If plans for the universal program proceed, the International Labour Organization will support the implementation process to be carried out jointly by the World Health Organization and the German Development Agency. In 2006, pending further action on the universal program, eligibility for the NHIF has been somewhat expanded.

ECONOMY

Overview: Kenya has one of Africa's worst performing economies, notwithstanding a pick-up of economic growth in the past three years. The economy is market-based, with some state-owned infrastructure enterprises, and maintains a liberalized external trade system. The economy's heavy dependence on rain-fed agriculture and the tourism sector leaves it vulnerable to cycles of boom and bust. The agricultural sector employs nearly 75 percent of the country's 37 million people. Half of the sector's output remains subsistence production.

Kenya's gross domestic product (GDP) growth rate declined continuously from a peak of about 6.5 percent per year during the first decade after independence to less than 4 percent per year in the following decade, to only about 1.5 percent per year during the 1990s. It has experienced an upturn to more than 5 percent per year since 2004. Several decades of declining economic performance, combined with rapid population growth, translated over time into reduced income per head, increased poverty, and worsening unemployment. Between the 1970s and 2000, the number of Kenyans classified as poor grew from 29 percent to about 57 percent.

Kenya's economic performance has been hampered by numerous interacting factors: heavy dependence on a few agricultural exports that are vulnerable to world price fluctuations, population growth that has outstripped economic growth, prolonged drought that has necessitated power rationing, deteriorating infrastructure, and extreme disparities of wealth that have limited the opportunities of most to develop their skills and knowledge. Poor governance and corruption also have had a negative impact on growth, making it expensive to do business in Kenya. According to Transparency International, Kenya ranks among the world's half-dozen most corrupt countries. Bribery and fraud cost Kenya as much as US$1 billion a year. Kenyans, 23 percent living on less than US$1 per day, pay some 16 bribes a month—two in every three encounters with public officials. Another large drag on Kenya's economy is the burden of human immunodeficiency virus/acquired immune deficiency syndrome (HIV/AIDS).

Prospects brightened somewhat under the Kibaki government, whose policy aims include budgetary reforms and debt restraint. Despite early disillusionment with the government, the economy has seen a broad-based expansion, led by strong performance in tourism and telecommunications, and acceptable post-drought results in agriculture, especially the vital tea sector. Nevertheless, risks to continuing robust growth remain, including weak infrastructure, drought, political instability in the run-up to the December 2007 elections, and diminution of financial flows from donors because of ongoing corruption allegations.

Gross Domestic Product (GDP): In 2006 Kenya's GDP was about US$17.39 billion. Per capita GDP averages somewhat more than US$450 annually. Adjusted in purchasing power parity (PPP) terms, per capita GDP in 2006 was about US$1,200. The country's real GDP growth picked up to 2.3 percent in early 2004 and to nearly 6 percent in 2005 and 2006, compared with a sluggish 1.4 percent in 2003 and throughout President Moi's last term (1997–2002). Real GDP is expected to continue to improve, largely because of expansions in tourism, telecommunications, transport, and construction and a recovery in agriculture. The Kenya Central Bank forecast for 2007 is between 5 and 6 percent GDP growth. GDP composition by sector, according to 2004 estimates, was as follows: agriculture, 25.7 percent; manufacturing, 14.0 percent; trade, restaurants, and hotels, 13.8 percent; transport and communications, 6.9 percent; government services, 15.6 percent; and other, 24.0 percent.

Government Budget: The budgets of the Moi era (1978–2002) carried increasingly worrisome deficits, and the Kibaki government's first budget for fiscal year (FY) 2004 was similarly unbalanced. In 2006 Kenya's revenues totaled US$4.448 billion, while its estimated expenditures totaled US$5.377 billion. Government budget balance as a percentage of gross domestic product—a low –5.5 percent in 2004—had improved to –2.1 percent in 2006.

Inflation: In 2006 the inflation rate for consumer prices was estimated at 14.5 percent. This rate was a significant rise from the previous year's 10.3 percent, reflecting higher food prices, which carry a 50 percent weighting in the consumer price index.

Agriculture, Forestry, and Fishing: The agricultural sector continues to dominate Kenya's economy, although only 15 percent of Kenya's total land area has sufficient fertility and rainfall to be farmed, and only 7 or 8 percent can be classified as first-class land. In 2006 almost 75 percent of working Kenyans made their living on the land, compared with 80 percent in 1980.

About one-half of total agricultural output is non-marketed subsistence production. Agriculture is also the largest contributor to Kenya's gross domestic product (GDP). In 2005 agriculture, including forestry and fishing, accounted for about 24 percent of GDP, as well as for 18 percent of wage employment and 50 percent of revenue from exports. The principal cash crops are tea, horticultural produce, and coffee; horticultural produce and tea are the main growth sectors and the two most valuable of all of Kenya's exports. In 2005 horticulture accounted for 23 percent and tea for 22 percent of total export earnings. Coffee has declined in importance with depressed world prices, accounting for just 5 percent of export receipts in 2005. The production of major food staples such as corn is subject to sharp weather-related fluctuations. Production downturns periodically necessitate food aid—for example, in 2004 aid for 1.8 million people—because of one of Kenya's intermittent droughts.

Tea, coffee, sisal, pyrethrum, corn, and wheat are grown in the fertile highlands, one of the most successful agricultural production regions in Africa. Production is mainly on small African-owned farms formed from the division of formerly European-owned estates. Livestock predominates in the semi-arid savanna to the north and east. Coconuts, pineapples, cashew nuts, cotton, sugarcane, sisal, and corn are grown in the lower-lying areas.

Forestry and Fishing: Resource degradation has reduced output from forestry. In 2004 roundwood removals came to 22,162,000 cubic meters. Fisheries are of local importance around Lake Victoria and have potential on Lake Turkana. Kenya's total catch reported in 2004 was 128,000 metric tons. However, output from fishing has been declining because of ecological disruption. Pollution, overfishing, and the use of unauthorized fishing equipment have led to falling catches and have endangered local fish species.

Mining and Minerals: Kenya has no significant mineral endowment. The mining and quarrying sector makes a negligible contribution to the economy, accounting for less than 1 percent of gross domestic product, the majority contributed by the soda ash operation at Lake Magadi in south-central Kenya. Thanks largely to rising soda ash output, Kenya's mineral production in 2005 reached more than 1 million tons. One of Kenya's largest foreign-investment projects in recent years is the planned expansion of Magadi Soda. Apart from soda ash, the chief minerals produced are limestone, gold, salt, and fluorspar.

All unextracted minerals are government property, according to the Mining Act. The Department of Mines and Geology, under the Ministry of Environment and Natural Resources, controls exploration and exploitation of such minerals.

Industry and Manufacturing: Although Kenya is the most industrially developed country in East Africa, manufacturing still accounts for only 14 percent of gross domestic product (GDP). This level of manufacturing GDP represents only a slight increase since independence. Expansion of the sector after independence, initially rapid, has stagnated since the 1980s, hampered by shortages in hydroelectric power, high energy costs, dilapidated transport infrastructure, endemic corruption, and the dumping of cheap imports. Industrial activity, concentrated around the three largest urban centers, Nairobi, Mombasa, and Kisumu, is dominated by food-processing industries such as grain milling, beer production, and sugarcane crushing, and the fabrication of consumer goods, e.g., vehicles from kits. Kenya also has an oil refinery that processes imported crude petroleum into petroleum products, mainly for the domestic market. In addition, a substantial and expanding informal sector engages in small-scale manufacturing of household goods, motor-vehicle parts, and farm implements. About half of the investment in the industrial sector is foreign, with the United Kingdom providing half. The United States is the second largest investor.

Kenya's inclusion among the beneficiaries of the U.S. Government's African Growth and Opportunity Act (AGOA) has given a boost to manufacturing in recent years. Since AGOA took effect in 2000, Kenya's clothing sales to the United States increased from US$44 million to US$270 million (2006). Other initiatives to strengthen manufacturing have been the new government's favorable tax measures, including the removal of duty on capital equipment and other raw materials.

Energy: The largest share of Kenya's electricity supply comes from hydroelectric stations at dams along the upper Tana River, as well as the Turkwel Gorge Dam in the west. A petroleum-fired plant on the coast, geothermal facilities at Olkaria (near Nairobi), and electricity imported from Uganda make up the rest of the supply. Kenya's installed capacity stood at 1,142 megawatts a year between 2001 and 2003. The state-owned Kenya Electricity Generating Company (KenGen), established in 1997 under the name of Kenya Power Company, handles the generation of electricity, while the Kenya Power and Lighting Company (KPLC), which is slated for privatization, handles transmission and distribution. Shortfalls of electricity occur periodically, when drought reduces water flow. In 1997 and 2000, for example, drought prompted severe power rationing, with economically damaging 12-hour blackouts. Frequent outages, as well as high cost, remain serious obstacles to economic activity. Tax and other concessions are planned to encourage investment in hydroelectricity and in geothermal energy, in which Kenya is a pioneer. The government plans to open two new power stations in 2008, Sondu Miriu (hydroelectric) and Olkaria IV (geothermal), but power demand growth is strong, and demand is still expected to outpace supply during periods of drought.

Kenya has yet to find hydrocarbon reserves on its territory, despite several decades of intermittent exploration. Although Australia continues the search off Kenya's shore, Kenya currently imports all crude petroleum requirements. Petroleum accounts for 20 to 25 percent of the national import bill. Kenya Petroleum Refineries—a 50:50 joint venture between the government and several oil majors—operates the country's sole oil refinery in Mombasa, which currently meets 60 percent of local demand for petroleum products. In 2004 oil consumption was estimated at 55,000 barrels a day. Most of the Mombasa refinery's production is transported via Kenya's Mombasa–Nairobi pipeline.

Services: Kenya's services sector, which contributes about 63 percent of GDP, is dominated by tourism. The tourism sector has exhibited steady growth in most years since independence and by the late 1980s had become the country's principal source of foreign exchange. In the late 1990s, tourism relinquished this position to tea exports, because of a terrorism-related downturn. The downturn followed the 1998 bombing of the U.S Embassy in Nairobi and later negative travel advisories from Western governments. Tourists, the largest number from Germany and the United Kingdom, are attracted mainly to the coastal beaches and the game parks, notably, the expansive Tsavo National Park (20,808 square kilometers) in the southeast. The government and

12

tourist industry organizations have taken steps to address the security problem and to reverse negative publicity. Such steps include establishing a tourist police and launching marketing campaigns in key tourist origin markets. Tourism has seen a substantial revival over the past several years and is the major contributor to the pick-up in the country's economic growth.

Tourism is now Kenya's largest foreign exchange earning sector, followed by flowers, tea, and coffee. In 2006 tourism generated US$803 million, up from US$699 million the previous year.

Other elements of Kenya's services sector face challenges of downsizing, in particular, the financial system. The Kenya banking system is supervised by the Central Bank of Kenya (CBK). As of late July 2004, the system consisted of 43 commercial banks (down from 48 in 2001), several non-bank financial institutions, including mortgage companies, four savings and loan associations, and several score foreign-exchange bureaus. Two of the four largest banks, the Kenya Commercial Bank (KCB) and the National Bank of Kenya (NBK), are partially government-owned, and the other two are majority foreign-owned (Barclays Bank and Standard Chartered). Most of the many smaller banks are family-owned and -operated.

Labor: In the early 2000s, agriculture remains the population's main occupation and source of income. In 2006 Kenya's labor force was estimated to include about 12 million workers, almost 75 percent in agriculture. The number employed outside small-scale agriculture and pastoralism was about 6 million. In 2004 about 15 percent of the labor force was officially classified as unemployed. Other estimates place Kenya's unemployment much higher, even up to 40 percent.

Foreign Economic Relations: Since independence, Kenya, a nonaligned but pro-Western country, has seen both substantial foreign investment and significant amounts of development aid, some from the communist bloc, most from the West. Between 60 and 70 percent of industry is still owned from abroad. Development assistance has come from increasingly diverse sources in recent years. The share provided by the United Kingdom has fallen, while that of multilateral agencies, particularly the World Bank and the European Development Fund, has increased. When President Moi left office in December 2002, one of the major concerns of international donors was removed, and they prepared to step up aid. The International Monetary Fund resumed aid after a three-year gap, and others followed suit with pledges of US$4.1 billion from 2004 to 2006 for development and budgetary support. By February 2005, however, relations with donors were again deteriorating, and some promised aid was suspended because of disappointing progress in tackling corruption and in instituting economic reforms, including privatization.

Aside from ties with advanced economies and donors, Kenya is active within regional trade blocs such as the Common Market for Eastern and Southern Africa (COMESA) and the East African Community (EAC), a partnership of Kenya, Uganda, and Tanzania. The EAC, dissolved in 1977 because of political tensions, was revived in 1997. The ultimate aim of the EAC is to create a common market of the three states modeled on the European Union. Among the early steps toward integration is the customs union of 2004, which eventually will eliminate duties on goods and non-tariff trade barriers among the members. The question of how the EAC will relate to other regional trade blocs, including COMESA and the Southern African Development Community (SADC), is in flux.

Imports and Exports: Kenya's chief exports are horticultural products and tea. In 2005 the combined value of these commodities was US$1,150 million, about 10 times the value of Kenya's third most valuable export, coffee. Kenya's other significant exports are petroleum products, sold to near neighbors, fish, cement, pyrethrum, and sisal. The leading imports are crude petroleum, chemicals, manufactured goods, machinery, and transportation equipment. Africa is Kenya's largest export market, followed by the European Union. The major destinations for exports are the United Kingdom (UK), Tanzania, Uganda, and the Netherlands. Major suppliers are the UK, United Arab Emirates, Japan, and India. Kenya's main exports to the United States are garments traded under the terms of the African Growth and Opportunity Act (AGOA). Despite AGOA, Kenya's apparel industry is struggling to hold its ground against Asian competition and runs a trade deficit with the United States.

Trade Balance: Kenya typically has a substantial trade deficit. The trade balance fluctuates widely because Kenya's main exports are primary commodities subject to the effects of both world prices and weather. In 2005 Kenya's income from exports was about US$3.2 billion. The payment for imports was about US$5.7 billion, yielding a trade deficit of about US$2.5 billion.

Balance of Payments: In 2006 Kenya had a current account deficit of US$1.5 billion. This figure was a significant increase over 2005, when the current account had a deficit of US$495 million. In 2006 the current account balance as a percentage of gross domestic product was –4.2.

External Debt: In 2006 Kenya's external debt totaled US$6.7 billion. The debt is forecast to be a manageable 30 percent of gross domestic product in 2007.

Foreign Investment: Kenyan policies on foreign investment generally have been favorable since independence, with occasional tightening of restrictions to promote the "Africanization" of enterprises. Foreign investors have been guaranteed ownership and the right to remit dividends, royalties, and capital. In the 1970s, the government disallowed foreign investment unless there was also some government participation in the ownership of an enterprise. Notwithstanding some restrictions, between 60 and 70 percent of industry is still owned from abroad. The most active investors have been the British.

Currency and Exchange Rate: The value of the Kenya shilling (KSh), Kenya's unit of currency, declined during President Moi's last term (1997–2002) from about KSh60 per US$1 in 1998 to KSh78.75 per US$1 in 2002. The exchange rate of the Kenya shilling between 2003 and 2005 averaged about KSh76 to US$1. As of June 1, 2007, the rate was KSh67=US$1.

Fiscal Year: Kenya's fiscal year runs from July 1 though June 30.

TRANSPORTATION AND TELECOMMUNICATIONS

Overview: Road, rail, and air transport are all significant in Kenya, while water transport plays a minor role. All of Kenya's transportation sectors, but particularly road and rail, are in need of stepped-up investment for better maintenance and expansion.

Roads: Kenya has an extensive 64,000-kilometer road network, about 8,000 kilometers of which are paved. The roads, which carry more than 80 percent of passenger and freight traffic, offer increasing coverage of all parts of the country. However, serious under-investment and corruption in contracts have left the road network in a poor state of repair. This poor condition contributes to an appalling rate of road accidents and deaths, the highest in the world. Road safety is further reduced by the operation of 25,000 *matutas* (minibuses), which constitute about 78 percent of the country's public transport system. Aiming to cut carnage on the roads, the Kibaki government in February 2004 obliged *matuta* owners to install safety equipment, a measure that led to sharp fare increases and overcrowded trains. The government and donor countries have prioritized the rehabilitation of the road infrastructure as a key part of the country's development strategy. In April 2004, the World Bank approved funding of US$207 million to support the Northern Corridor Transport Improvement (NCTI) project, 80 percent of which will be spent on roads. Other funds will come from private capital offset by toll charges, as well as donations from the European Union and the United States.

Railroads: Kenya's railroad system has about 2,778 kilometers of narrow-gauge, one-meter track, 150 stations, and a fleet of 156 locomotives and some 7,000 coaches and wagons, including container-carrying Railtrainers. The system, managed by the Kenya Railway Corporation (KRC), serves both Kenya and land-locked countries in the East African region. The most important route runs from Mombasa through Nairobi to the Ugandan border. Kenya also has commuter rail that serves the Nairobi suburbs. In 2004 Kenya and Uganda approved a merger of their railroad corporations and jointly offered the merged railroad for concession to private operators/investors. In 2006 the winning concessionaire was Rift Valley Railways (RVR), a consortium led by South Africa's Sheltam Rail Company. RVR acquired rights to 1,920 kilometers of track in Kenya, which carried an average of 2.3 million tons of freight and 4.7 million passengers per year between fiscal year (FY) 2000 and FY 2003.

Ports: Kenya's port traffic climbed to 14.4 million metric tons of freight in 2006. The principal seaport, Mombasa, is the main sea outlet for both inland Kenya and the land-locked countries of East and Central Africa, e.g., Uganda, Rwanda, Burundi, the eastern Democratic Republic of the Congo, and southern Sudan. The Kenya Ports Authority (KPA), created in 1978, manages port operations at Mombasa, as well as inland container depots in Nairobi, Eldoret, and Kisumu. The KPA also has jurisdiction over the small ports of Lamu, Kiunga, Kilifi, Malindi, Funzi, Mtwapa, Shimoni, and Vanga. Mombasa is a deep-water port with 21 berths that can handle all sizes of ships and 300,000 containers per year. Freight handled through Mombasa jumped by 12.6 percent in 2003, but inefficiencies, corruption, and deteriorating infrastructure at the port continue to be cited as a major deterrent to business in Kenya. There are plans to refurbish some of the port's equipment.

Inland Waterways: Water transport is the least used mode of transportation in Kenya, limited to the coastal and lake regions. The only significant inland waterway is the part of Lake Victoria within the boundaries of Kenya. The Kenya Railways Corporation (KRC) operates ferry services there to link Ugandan and Tanzanian locations with Kisumu, Kenya's third largest town and a once bustling port. The ferry supplements interstate rail and road traffic. In addition to the ferry, the KRC has two freight tugs, nine lighter barges, and three passenger vessels on Lake Victoria.

Civil Aviation and Airports: Kenya has more than 200 airports and airfields, 15 of which have paved runways, including four with runways longer than 3,000 meters. About 35 airfields can be considered commercial. Three airports handle international flights, Nairobi's Jomo Kenyatta International Airport (JKIA), Mombasa's Moi International Airport (MIA), and Eldoret International Airport. Other facilities include Wilson Airport in Nairobi; airports at Malindi, Kakuma, and Kisumu; and numerous airstrips throughout the country. The Northern Corridor Transport Improvement (NCTI) project approved in mid-2004 includes US$41 million for aviation. The funds are earmarked to enhance facilities and safety at JKIA and MIA, including perimeter fencing and new navigation, security, and baggage-handling equipment. The runway extension at JKIA will raise capacity from 2.5 to 5.5 million passengers per year. A key objective of the airport upgrade is to win "category one" status from the U.S. Federal Aviation Administration to allow for direct flights between JKIA and U.S. airports. Direct flights would boost tourism and trade and secure JKIA's status as a regional hub.

Pipelines: The Kenya Pipeline Company (KPC), a state-owned enterprise (parastatal) formed in 1973, transports about 90 percent of the petroleum products consumed in Kenya's domestic market. The KPC owns and operates the Mombasa–Nairobi pipeline, whose throughput has risen because of restrictions imposed on the road transport of petroleum to stem the diversion of supplies to local markets. A second pipeline stretches from Eldoret to Kisumu in the west of the country, and a recent project is to extend the pipeline from Eldoret to Kampala in Uganda, under the auspices of the East African Community. The KPC is the dominant player in the regional energy sector, exporting to Uganda, Tanzania, Rwanda, Burundi, the Democratic Republic of the Congo, and Sudan.

Telecommunications: This sector, a key to sustained economic development in Kenya, experienced rapid growth in 2000–2006 because of the proliferation of mobile cellular telephones. The number of cell phone subscribers increased from 24,000 in 1999 to 5 million in 2005. In 2005 Kenya's telephone landlines numbered 282,000, compared with 106,000 in 1984. The landline system has been generally unreliable, having seen little modernization except for service to businesses. The burgeoning cellular phone system is operated by two license holders, Safaricom and Celtel, to be joined eventually by a third, Econet Wireless Kenya. Internet use also has expanded rapidly, reaching 1 million by 2005. The country had six television broadcast stations in 2007 and more than three dozen radio stations. Kenya is estimated to have 22 televisions per 1,000 people.

GOVERNMENT AND POLITICS

Political System Overview: Kenya is a republic dominated by a strong presidency. The political system is in flux as contentious debate continues on efforts to adopt a new constitution. A popular referendum in 2005 defeated a proposed constitution supported by the government. The constitution to be replaced was drawn up at independence. This constitution, heavily indebted to English law, has already been amended more than 30 times but is widely agreed to require a major overhaul. The constitution gives the president wide-ranging powers, provides for no prime minister, and is ill-suited to multiparty politics, despite the 1991 repeal of a section that had formalized the one-party state. Key proposals in the recently defeated draft constitution called for

16

reducing the powers vested in the office of the president, providing for a prime minister, and ensuring the independence of the judiciary.

Besides the constitution, a pressing concern in Kenyan politics is corruption. Recent anticorruption efforts have led to the establishment of the Kenya Anti-Corruption Commission (KACC) and to laws requiring civil servants to disclose assets and mandating transparency in procurement. The government also promised to trace ill-gotten assets and has set up commissions to unravel the decades-old illegal allocation of public lands and a major corruption scandal from the 1990s, the Goldenberg Affair. Despite such anticorruption activity, Kenya's anticorruption campaign, in the perception of most Kenyans surveyed, has stagnated.

Executive Branch: Under Kenya's current constitution, the president is both the chief of state and head of government. The president is elected by popular vote for a five-year term, with the possibility of re-election to a second term. The presidential candidate must receive the largest number of votes in absolute terms and also, in order to avoid a runoff, must win 25 percent or more of the vote in at least five of Kenya's seven provinces and the Nairobi area. The president appoints the vice president and members of the cabinet, who must be members of the National Assembly. The president also exercises direct control over the key areas of security and defense and has extensive powers over the appointment of the attorney general, the chief justice of the Court of Appeal, and Court of Appeal and High Court judges.

Legislative Branch: Kenya's National Assembly, or Bunge, is a unicameral legislature with 224 members, 210 of whom are elected by popular vote for five-year terms. The president appoints 12 "nominated" members, who are selected by the parties in proportion to the votes the parties receive in parliamentary elections. Two members serve ex-officio.

Judicial Branch: Kenya's court hierarchy consists of the Court of Appeal, High Court, resident and district magistrates' courts, and *kadhis* courts, which adjudicate Muslim personal law concerning personal status, marriage, divorce, and inheritance among Muslims. Kenya's president appoints judges, including the chief justice, who presides in the Court of Appeal. The High Court is responsible for judicial review. Kenya accepts compulsory International Court of Justice jurisdiction, with reservations. The judiciary is constitutionally independent, and judges have security of tenure. This constitutional status and the theoretical life tenure of judges have not, however, ensured immunity from executive-branch pressure.

Administrative Divisions: Kenya is divided into seven provinces and the Nairobi Area. The provinces are Central, Coast, Eastern, North-Eastern, Nyanza, Rift Valley, and Western. Lower-level administrative units include 40 districts and further subdivisions.

Provincial and Local Government: The seven provinces and the Nairobi Area are administered by provincial commissioners who are answerable to the president. Elective municipal, town, and county councils have limited powers delegated by the national government. Important council officials such as the town clerk and treasurer all are appointed by the central government in Nairobi.

Judicial and Legal System: Kenya's legal system is based on Kenyan statutory law, Kenyan and English common law, tribal law, and Islamic law. Bias and corruption in the court system frequently compromise the right to a fair trial. In 2003, following the resignation of the chief justice, the anticorruption authority found credible evidence of corruption against five of nine Court of Appeal judges and proof of misconduct against 18 of 36 High Court judges and 82 of 254 magistrates. In October 2003, one-half of Kenya's senior judges were suspended over allegations of corruption, and tribunals were established to investigate the charges against them. Many of the judges resigned rather than face tribunals.

Electoral System: Suffrage in Kenya is universal at age 18. National presidential and parliamentary elections are held every five years. Election is by a plurality of votes. The most recent elections for president and for parliament were held in December 2002 and will next be held in late 2007.

Politics and Political Parties: Multiparty politics reemerged in Kenya after December 1991, with the repeal of Section 2a of the constitution. In 1982 Section 2a had officially made Kenya a one-party state, with the Kenya African National Union (KANU) the sole legal party. Kenya had been a de facto one-party state since 1969. As of that date, all political candidates had to be members of KANU. The reemergence of a multiparty system in the 1990s initially produced a fractured opposition to President Moi and KANU. After 1991 an important new opposition party, the Forum for the Restoration of Democracy (FORD), soon split into factions, and numerous other parties emerged. After two national elections in which Moi won against divided opposition, various opposition elements formed the National Rainbow Coalition (NARC), a coalition of a dozen parties, including the National Alliance of Kenya (NAK) and the Liberal Democratic Party (LDP). NARC ran Mwai Kibaki as its candidate for president in 2002 and won a solid victory to become the governing party. Several years after the election, NARC broke up over disagreements about the draft constitution. Some constituent elements of NARC joined KANU to form a new opposition coalition, the Orange Democratic Movement, while other elements became part of a new pro-Kibaki group, NARC–Kenya.

Mass Media: Kenya's state-owned Kenya Broadcasting Corporation remains the only broadcaster with countrywide coverage. A dozen private radio and television stations have ranges that are limited to the Nairobi area. A number of recently established private radio stations broadcast in local languages, including Kameme FM (Kikuyu), Metro East FM (Hindi), and Rehema Radio (Kalenjin). More than 100 applications for radio and television licenses are pending before the government-controlled Communication Commission of Kenya. Kenya's print media are diverse, ranging from well-respected newspapers and magazines to an expansive tabloid press. Two independent national newspapers, the *Daily Nation* and *The Standard*, feature quality reporting, as does the weekly, *The East African*, which is published in Nairobi, as well as in Dar es Salaam and Kampala.

Under the Kibaki government, the media have demonstrated greater editorial independence than in previous years, and the number of press freedom abuses has declined. Still, some media policies and incidents continue to inhibit press freedom, e.g., the need to post a costly bond prior to publication and to register afterward. In 2003 the government invoked a restrictive constitutional provision on court coverage to intimidate journalists reporting on a possible political murder. In March 2006, hooded policemen raided the offices of *The Standard* newspaper and Kenya Television Network, claiming concerns about internal security.

Foreign Relations: Under Jomo Kenyatta (1963–78), one of the more pro-British of African leaders, Kenya was officially nonaligned but set a pattern of friendly relations with the West. The United Kingdom (UK), the former colonial power, provided assistance to smooth Kenya's transition to black majority rule by compensating white settlers. Kenya permitted the UK to use its hinterlands for military training. An important foreign relations development under President Moi was Kenya's support of U.S. military commitments in the Indian Ocean. This support has gained renewed importance since the Horn of Africa became a front line in the fight against terrorism. The ongoing threat of terrorist attacks by Islamists in the area stands to cement the country's close ties with the United States.

In addition to its ties with Western powers, Kenya is a major player regionally, taking an active role in the affairs of its neighbors. At various times, Kenya has had conflicts with each of the five neighbors over, for example, boundaries, border incursions, harboring rebels, interfering with cross-border traffic flow, and the use of Nile waters. Diplomatic and mediation efforts, often spearheaded by Kenya, typically have eased the conflicts. Most recently, for instance, Kenya helped in peace talks that aimed to end the civil war in southern Sudan, along with the war's spillover effects in Kenya. The most intractable problems at present are with unstable Somalia, which claims a restive Somali-populated part of Kenya and is a source of outlaws, refugees, hostile craft, and, possibly, terrorists. Concerned about Islamist strength in Somalia, Kenya lent indirect support to the military campaign waged in Somalia in December 2006 by Ethiopia and Somalia's Transitional Federal Government against the Union of Islamic Courts militia. In January 2007, Kenya closed its border with Somalia in order to exclude the routed Islamists. More positive relations between Kenya and its neighbors, namely, Uganda and Tanzania, are currently developing through the relaunch of the tripartite trade bloc, the East African Community (EAC), as well as the broader organization, the Common Market for Eastern and Southern Africa (COMESA).

Membership in International Organizations: Kenya is a member of numerous international organizations whose focus is primarily Africa, including the Africa Development Bank (AfDB); African Union (AU); Common Market for Eastern and Southern Africa (COMESA); Cotonou Convention; East African Community (EAC); Indian Ocean Rim Association for Regional Co-operation (IOR–ARC); and Intergovernmental Authority on Development (IGAD). Some of Kenya's other major memberships, which have a broader international focus, include the Food and Agriculture Organization of the United Nations (FAO); Group of 15; Group of 77; International Atomic Energy Agency (IAEA); International Bank for Reconstruction and Development (IBRD); International Civil Aviation Organization (ICAO); International Criminal Police Organization (Interpol); International Fund for Agricultural Development (IFAD); International Labour Organization (ILO); International Maritime Organization (IMO); International Monetary Fund (IMF); International Organization for Migration (IOM); International Telecommunication Union (ITU); Organisation for the Prohibition of Chemical Weapons (OPCW); United Nations (UN); United Nations Committee on Trade and Development (UNCTAD); United Nations Educational, Scientific, and Cultural Organization (UNESCO); United Nations Office of the High Commissioner for Refugees (UNHCR); United Nations

Industrial Development Organization (UNIDO); Universal Postal Union (UPU); World Health Organization (WHO); World Intellectual Property Organization (WIPO); World Meteorological Organization (WMO); and World Trade Organization (WTO).

Major International Treaties: Kenya has acceded to major international treaties, accords, and conventions in many areas, for example, human rights, the environment, and nonproliferation. The environmental agreements include some 16 global and regional accords on the atmosphere, hazardous substances, marine resources, and living resources of the sea, freshwater, and land. Kenya has signed major conventions regarding nuclear safety and biological, chemical, and nuclear weapons, as well as the Convention on the Prohibition of the Use, Stockpiling, Production and Transfer of Anti-Personnel Mines and on their Destruction. Kenya is a signatory to most of the major international human rights treaties, for example: Economic, Social and Cultural Rights in 1972; Civil and Political Rights in 1972; Discrimination Against Women in 1984; Torture in 1997; and Rights of the Child in 1990.

NATIONAL SECURITY

Armed Forces Overview: In mid-2006, regular armed forces totaled 24,120 active personnel, including headquarters staff. The army numbered 20,000; the navy, 1,620 (including 120 marines); and the air force, 2,500. Kenya's military participates regularly in international operations and exercises. Kenya also has a paramilitary internal security force, the 5,000-strong General Service Unit (GSU), which is part of the police. Among police units, the GSU is the most notorious for human rights abuses. The rest of the police has a reputation for graft.

Foreign Military Relations: Kenya long has had informal military alliances with the United States and the United Kingdom (UK). Since 1980 Kenya has supported U.S. military commitments in the Indian Ocean by permitting the use of Mombasa port and air base facilities in exchange for U.S. military assistance. The U.S. Central Command—which covers the Middle East, Central Asia, and the Horn of Africa—has not sought permanent basing rights in Kenya because of the availability of Djibouti. However, Kenya is a valuable point of entry and staging platform, for example, for U.S., British, and German aerial and naval search operations targeting al-Qaeda–linked Somalia-based groups. U.S. and British forces also use Kenyan territory for training, the UK since before Kenyan independence. The UK conducts three to four military exercises per year in remote areas, often with Kenyan participation. In recent years, the United States has provided joint peace support training through its Africa Crisis Response Initiative (ACRI) program, as well as conventional military training under the Africa Contingency Operations Training Assistance (ACOTA) program. A major amphibious joint exercise, "Edged Mallet," is held regularly along the northern Kenyan coast and has involved up to 3,000 U.S. Marines. In 2004 the joint exercise had regional terrorism as the primary focus.

Currently, Kenyan and U.S. officials are discussing a new U.S. military command, Africa Command (AFRICOM), which will oversee U.S. military operations in Africa. Announced in 2007, AFRICOM will be carved out of the three combatant commands responsible for the continent: European Command, Central Command, and Pacific Command. AFRICOM will stand up initially in Germany at European Command headquarters and become fully established in late

2008 somewhere in Africa. Kenya is among the 10 countries being considered for AFRICOM's main base.

External Threat: Kenya has security concerns regarding several near neighbors, chiefly, Somalia, Sudan, and Uganda. Somalia poses a threat in the disputed and lawless semi-desert northeastern region of Kenya, where there is a large Somali ethnic population. In the early 1990s, this population was augmented by a large Somali refugee influx fleeing political breakdown in Somalia. The Somali frontier is porous to illegal weapons traffic and other contraband and to livestock raiders and bandits, as well as to potential terrorists. In response to the crisis in Somalia in 2006, Kenya deployed its forces along its border with Somalia and at sea to apprehend extremist Somali fighters fleeing the Ethiopian advance and to prevent them from establishing safe haven in Kenya.

Sudan and Kenya have had a strained security relationship since the late 1980s. The Sudanese government accused Kenya of aiding the rebel Sudan People's Liberation Army (SPLA). Sudan also worries that Kenya could allow the United States to use it as a platform for actions against terrorists in Sudan. Further strains stem from Khartoum's claim to the "Elemi Triangle"—a potentially oil-rich arid area on the Kenyan side of the border. Despite the tensions, Kenya has played a leading role as a mediator in Sudan's civil war. Bilateral relations between Uganda and Kenya periodically also have been strained, with mutual concerns about cross-border incursions and arms provision to dissidents, as well as fears about Kenyan interference with transport and Ugandan cutoff of electricity supplies.

Defense Budget: Kenya's military expenditures for 2005 totaled US$280.5 million, which represented 3 percent of gross domestic product (GDP), an increase from 1999, when expenditures constituted 1.9 percent of GDP.

Major Military Units: As of 2006, Kenya's military had five brigades: two infantry, one with three battalions and one with two battalions; one armored, with three battalions; one artillery, with two battalions; and one engineer, with two battalions. In addition, the army includes the following four battalions: air defense artillery, airborne, independent infantry, and independent air cavalry.

Major Military Equipment: As of 2006, the army had 78 main battle tanks, 92 reconnaissance vehicles, 62 armored personnel carriers, 48 pieces of towed artillery, 62 mortars, 54 antitank guided weapons, 80 recoilless launchers, and 94 air defense guns. The navy had four offshore patrol craft, two amphibious craft, and one support craft. The air force had 9 combat aircraft, 34 attack helicopters (of doubtful serviceability), 30 transport aircraft, 17 transport helicopters, 25 training aircraft, and various missiles.

Military Service: Recruitment into the armed forces is on a voluntary basis. The minimum recruitment age is 18. The recruit must be a Kenyan citizen and have a national identity card, which may be issued only when the applicant is 18 and is able to produce a birth certificate. In 2005 persons in the eligible age-group of 18 to 49 numbered 7,303,000 males and 7,084,000 females.

Paramilitary Forces: In addition to the regular armed forces and the regular national police, the government can call on a special security force, the 5,000-strong General Service Unit (GSU). Part of the police but semi-autonomous, the GSU acts as the uniformed paramilitary cousin of the security and intelligence units. The GSU handles violent crime, outbreaks of communal violence, and demonstrations. Since 2003, the GSU also has had certain counterterrorism functions, including patrolling around Kenya's international airports. The GSU has 12 boats, an air wing of seven light, fixed-wing aircraft and three helicopters, and eight armored cars. In carrying out its functions, the GSU is especially notorious among police units for human rights violations, including extrajudicial killings and torture.

Military Forces Abroad: Since 1989, Kenya has participated in more than 20 United Nations peacekeeping operations worldwide, contributing military observers, staff officers, police monitors, and infantry troops. Kenya is the third largest African contributor of troops to such operations, after Nigeria and Ghana. Kenyan forces have deployed for missions in numerous African countries, in the Balkans, and in East Timor. Currently, Kenya contributes forces to the African Union's peacekeeping operations in Darfur, Sudan. Kenya also contributed personnel to the U.S.-led coalition forces operating in Afghanistan after October 7, 2001.

Police: Kenya Police, a national civilian force about 30,000 strong, is divided into a number of separate operational units, including an air wing, port police for the Indian Ocean and Lake Victoria, and a Criminal Investigation Department (CID) intelligence division, which investigates criminal activity. An Anti-Corruption Unit, created in August 2001, reports to the CID director. Another element of Kenya's large internal security apparatus is the National Security Intelligence Service (NSIS), the primary civilian intelligence organization. The NSIS was established in 1998 from the Police Special Branch (Security Intelligence Service) to monitor people considered subversive. The NSIS's formation was spurred by the August 1998 U.S. embassy bombing. In the aftermath of the bombing investigation, U.S. Federal Bureau of Investigation (FBI) agents and other consultants stayed on to help train the NSIS in urban counterinsurgency and counterterrorism strategy. With the victory of Mwai Kibaki in the presidential election in December 2002, further steps were taken to professionalize the NSIS, including the initiation in 2003 of a graduate training program. A Tourism Police Unit, with an initial contingent of 450 officers, also was established in mid-2003, with the charge of reducing concerns about the threat to foreign tourists from terrorism, especially in Coast Province. The various new police units augment the internal security capabilities that were long the province of the paramilitary General Service Unit.

Internal Threat: A relatively stable country, Kenya's political status quo is not under significant threat either from its own security forces or from rebel political movements. Kenya's nearest brush with a military coup occurred in 1982 in a brief failed action by air force officers. No local insurgencies of consequence currently exist. Kenya's chief sources of internal unrest are ethnic tensions. Such tensions and flare-ups of interethnic violence frequently arise from competition for productive areas. Serious interethnic disturbances erupted in the Rift Valley after the elections of 1992 and 1998. The 1998 clashes may have displaced 300,000 people.

Another key security concern in Kenya is the escalating level of crime, both urban and rural. Urban areas, especially the capital, nicknamed "Nairobbery," are plagued by burglary, armed robbery, and vehicle hijackings. Police complicity in illegal activity is much in evidence. The most prevalent form of serious rural crime is armed livestock rustling. Rustling and brigand activity, often linked to ethnic feuds, have rendered much of the North-Eastern Province and parts of the Coast and Eastern Provinces virtually ungovernable. Other prevalent forms of rural crime, attacks on tourists and poaching, have intermittently been better controlled, in particular, by the British Special Air Service (SAS)-trained Kenya Wildlife Service (KWS).

Terrorism: Kenya's vulnerability to Islamic terrorists operating under the al-Qaeda banner has been demonstrated by several attacks. Kenya was attacked first in 1998 when a car bomb blew up the U.S. embassy in Nairobi, killing well over 200 people, mostly Kenyans, and again in 2002, when suicide bombers killed 15 people in the Israeli-owned Paradise Hotel in Kikambala near Mombasa, and when terrorists reportedly shot a missile at an Israeli airliner at Mombasa airport. The embassy bombing was one of the most serious attacks on American interests outside the United States. Warnings of further possible terrorist activity in Kenya in May 2003 led to a six-week suspension of commercial flights from the United Kingdom to Kenya and negative travel advisories by several Western countries. The advisories have since been withdrawn or, in the U.S. case, softened. The United States renewed travel warnings about Kenya on December 28, 2004.

Located in the Horn region, Kenya faces an ongoing threat of terrorist attacks. The 1998 and 2002 attacks, according to a recent United Nations report, were prepared by a Somalia-based al-Qaeda–linked group in neighboring Somalia, which is beset by a strong fundamentalist presence, weak rule of law, and arms smuggling from Yemen. Kenya's Somalia border area, with its ethnic Somali communities, and the long, poorly guarded Indian Ocean coastline remain potential entry points for outside extremists. Kenya's own Muslim community on the coast, while largely moderate, offers a potential foothold for terrorist infiltrators.

Under pressure from the West and anxious to revive tourism, Kenya has taken action against suspected Islamic extremists, detaining and interrogating dozens of people in several drives in 2003. In 2004 four Kenyans were charged with involvement in the Paradise Hotel attacks. The four were acquitted on murder charges, but one was rearrested and sentenced in 2007 to eight years' imprisonment on firearms charges. Several other terrorism-related cases have ended in acquittals or dropped charges. In 2007 Kenya transferred a suspected al-Qaeda operative to Guantanamo Bay and, possibly, other suspects into custody elsewhere, e.g., in Somalia.

Kenya has sought to improve its security apparatus and legal framework to fight terrorism. In January 2004, Kenya opened the new National Counter-Terrorism Center, the first of its kind in Africa. The center aims to improve security throughout the Horn of Africa by coordinating information. Kenya also formed an interagency Coastal Security Steering Committee. Generally cooperative with the United States, Kenya has been a beneficiary of the U.S. aid to, for example, train its Anti-Terror Police Unit and upgrade air and seaport security. The Kenyan military also has participated in training and operations with the 1,800-member, U.S.-sponsored Combined Joint Task Force–Horn of Africa (JTF–HOA), a task force created to disrupt transnational terrorist groups in the Horn of Africa region. Kenya's government has taken steps to combat money laundering and terrorist financing, with a pending money-laundering bill, guidelines issued by the Central Bank, and the closure of Charterhouse Bank. The government has made some progress on improving aviation security. However, efforts to enact counterterrorism legislation, underway since 2003, have as yet been unsuccessful. In 2006 the National Assembly shelved a long-pending antiterrorism bill in the face of criticism from human rights groups and Kenyan Muslim communities.

Human Rights: The Kibaki government has worked to improve the human rights environment in Kenya and has reduced the use of the legal system to harass government critics. The Moi administration consistently received international criticism of its record on human rights. Under Moi, security forces regularly subjected opposition leaders and pro-democracy activists to arbitrary arrest, detention without trial, abuse in custody, and lethal force. International donors and governments such as the United States, Germany, the United Kingdom, and Norway periodically broke off diplomatic relations and suspended aid allocations, pending human rights improvement. Under the new government, politically motivated human rights violations have diminished, but other serious human rights abuses persist, a great many at the hands of security forces, particularly the police. The police force is widely viewed as the most corrupt entity in the country, given to extorting bribes, complicity in criminal activity, and using excessive force against both criminal suspects and crowds. Most police who commit abuses still do so with impunity. Prison conditions remain life threatening. Apart from police and penal system abuses, infringements of rights in the course of legal proceedings are widespread, despite recent pressure on judicial personnel. Freedom of speech and of the press continue to be compromised through various forms of harassment of journalists and activists, such as the March 2006 police raids on facilities of the Kenya Television Network and *The Standard*, Kenya's oldest newspaper.

Violence and discrimination against women are rife. Women's property rights violations are prevalent, aggravating the fact that women, although constituting 80 percent of the agricultural labor force, own only about 5 percent of the land. The abuse of children, including in forced labor and prostitution, is a serious problem. Female genital mutilation (FGM) remains widespread, despite 2001 legislation against it for girls under 16. The abuse of women and girls, including early marriage and wife inheritance, is a factor in the spread of human immunodeficiency virus/acquired immune deficiency syndrome (HIV/AIDS).

Kenya made some progress in 2003, when it set up the Kenya National Human Rights Commission, with a mandate to ensure Kenya's compliance with international human rights standards. Also, parliament passed the Children's Act to ensure the protection of minors, as well as the Disability Act, outlawing discrimination against the disabled.

In 2007 Kenya, along with Ethiopia, the United States, and the Transitional Federal Government of Somalia, was implicated in a secret detention program for people who fled the fighting between the Union of Islamic Courts and the joint forces of the Transitional Federal Government and Ethiopia from December 2006 through January 2007. Kenyan security forces allegedly arrested at least 150 individuals at crossing points with Somalia, held them without charge, and transferred them for interrogation to detention facilities in Ethiopia.